Pickled Peppers

Mc Graw Hill Education

Bothell, WA • Chicago, IL • Columbus, OH • New York, NY

MHEonline.com

Send all inquiries to:
McGraw-Hill Education
8787 Orion Place
Columbus, OH 43240

ISBN: 978-0-07-667240-0
MHID: 0-07-667240-9

Printed in the United States of America

15 16 17 18 19 GPC 25 24 23

Pickled Peppers

Pickled Peppers

Table of Contents

One, Two, Buckle My Shoe ·················➤ 6
illustrated by Todd Bonita

Little Boy Blue ·····························➤ 8
illustrated by Kellie Lewis

Jack and Jill ······························➤ 10
illustrated by Suwin Chan

Humpty Dumpty ·························➤ 11
illustrated by Phyllis Harris

Little Bo Peep ···························➤ 12
illustrated by Paige Billin-Frye

Peter Piper ·······························➤ 13
illustrated by Michiyo Nelson

The Mulberry Bush ······················➤ 14
illustrated by Jack Ross

Hickory Dickory Dock ···················➤ 15
illustrated by Susan Despirito

Mary Had a Little Lamb ·················➤ 16
illustrated by Thomas Kern

Higglety, Pigglety, Pop ·······················➤ 17
illustrated by Kris Levy

Cobbler, Cobbler, Mend My Shoe ···············➤ 18
illustrated by Lydia Adamo

Twinkle, Twinkle, Little Star ·····················➤ 19
illustrated by Ishaan Sangani

Baa, Baa, Black Sheep ························➤ 20
illustrated by Margot Braswell

Teddy Bear, Teddy Bear ·······················➤ 21
illustrated by Mark Rodriguez

Wee Willie Winkie ····························➤ 22
illustrated by Anna Burke

One, Two, Buckle My Shoe

illustrated by Todd Bonita

One, two, buckle my shoe;

Three, four, shut the door;

Five, six, pick up sticks;

Seven, eight, lay them straight;

Nine, ten, a big, fat hen.

Little Boy Blue

illustrated by Kellie Lewis

Little Boy Blue,
Come blow your horn,
The sheep's in the meadow,
The cow's in the corn.
Where is the boy
Who looks after the sheep?

He's under a haystack
Fast asleep.
Will you wake him?
No, not I,
For, if I do,
He's sure to cry.

Jack and Jill

illustrated by **Suwin Chan**

Jack and Jill,
Went up the hill,
To fetch a pail of water;
Jack fell down,
And broke his crown,
And Jill came tumbling after.

Humpty Dumpty

illustrated by Phyllis Harris

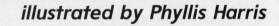

Humpty Dumpty sat on a wall,
Humpty Dumpty had a great fall;
All the King's horses and all the King's men
Couldn't put Humpty together again.

Little Bo Peep

illustrated by
Paige Billin-Frye

Little Bo Peep has lost her sheep,
And doesn't know where to find them.
Leave them alone,
and they'll come home,
Wagging their tails behind them.

Peter Piper

illustrated by Michiyo Nelson

Peter Piper picked
a peck of pickled peppers;
A peck of pickled peppers
Peter Piper picked.

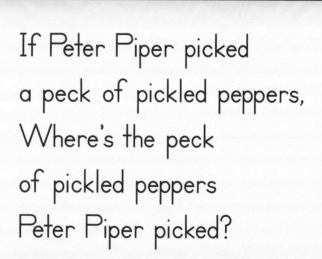

If Peter Piper picked
a peck of pickled peppers,
Where's the peck
of pickled peppers
Peter Piper picked?

The Mulberry Bush

illustrated by Jack Ross

Here we go 'round
the mulberry bush,
The mulberry bush,
the mulberry bush.

Here we go 'round
the mulberry bush,
So early Monday morning!

Hickory Dickory Dock

illustrated by
Susan Despirito

Hickory dickory dock,
The mouse ran up
  the clock,
The clock struck one,
The mouse ran down,
Hickory dickory dock.

Mary Had a Little Lamb

illustrated by Thomas Kern

Mary had a little lamb,
Its fleece was white as snow;
And everywhere that Mary went
The lamb was sure to go.

It followed her to school one day,
That was against the rule;
It made the children laugh and play
To see a lamb at school.

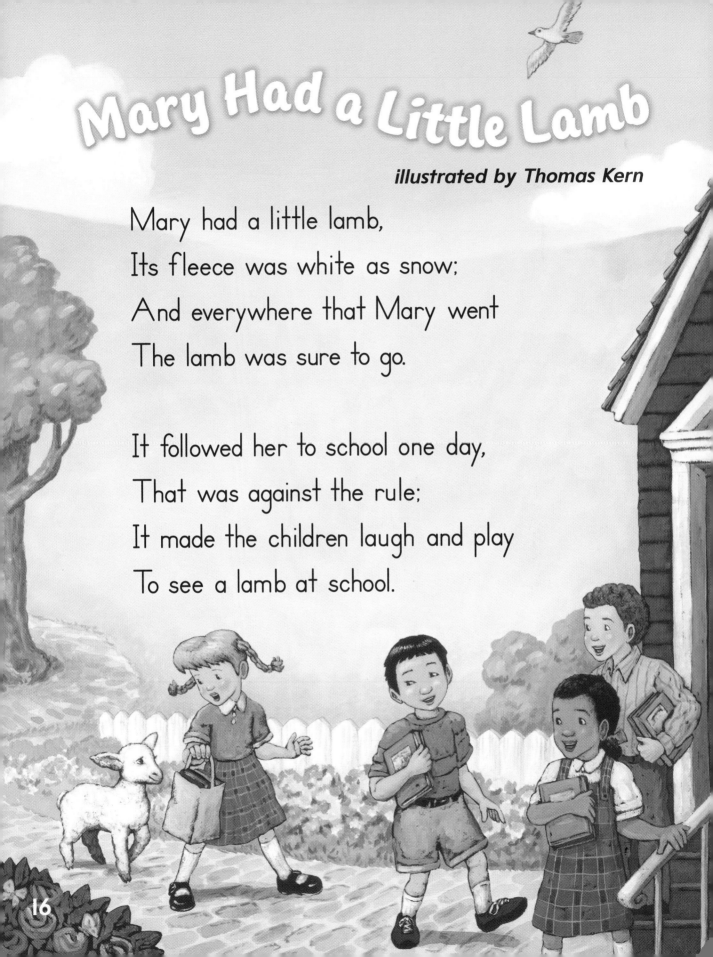

Higglety, Pigglety, POP

illustrated by Kris Levy

Higglety, pigglety, pop!
The dog has eaten the mop.
The pig's in a hurry,
The cat's in a flurry,
Higglety, pigglety, pop!

Cobbler, Cobbler, Mend My Shoe

illustrated by Lydia Adamo

Cobbler, cobbler, mend my shoe.

Get it done by half past two.

Half past two is much too late!

Get it done by half past eight.

Twinkle, Twinkle, Little Star

illustrated by Ishaan Sangani

Twinkle, twinkle, little star,

how I wonder what you are.

Up above the world so high,

like a diamond in the sky.

Twinkle, twinkle, little star,

how I wonder what you are.

Baa, Baa, Black Sheep

illustrated by Margot Braswell

Baa, baa, black sheep,
Have you any wool?
Yes sir, yes sir,
Three bags full.

One for the master,
One for the dame,
And one for the little boy
Who lives down the lane.

Teddy Bear, Teddy Bear

illustrated by Mark Rodriguez

Teddy Bear, Teddy Bear,
Turn around.
Teddy Bear, Teddy Bear,
Touch the ground.
Teddy Bear, Teddy Bear,
Tie your shoe.
Teddy Bear, Teddy Bear,
I love you.

Wee Willie Winkie

illustrated by Anna Burke

Wee Willie Winkie
  runs through the town,
Upstairs, downstairs,
  in his nightgown.
Rapping at the windows,
Crying through the lock;
"Are the children all in bed?
For now it's eight o'clock."